This Little Life

A Collection of Poems

by Elianna McHenry

Table of Contents

Dedication

Dedicated to my husband, Noah, for always encouraging me to fulfill my dreams even when they're crazy.

To my parents, Ken and Peggy, for providing a way for me to be creative in my writing even when I was young.

To my grandparents, Lyle and Betty, for always being every poem's biggest fans.

To my siblings, roommates, nieces and nephews and Ophelia for providing an awful lot of my material for so many of my projects.

About the Author

Elianna McHenry is a lover of words. A writer from a young age and a lover of her family. She is a wife, mother and a professor of accounting. Her writing material is often from her nieces, nephews, and other members of her family.

The Church

A church without little voices is old

A church without toys is old

A church without Cheerios is old

A church without giggles and cries is old

A church without crayons and paper is old

A church without tiny feet pattering is old

A church that is old will eventually die

The church is not a building, but it is the people

Baby Fever

Boy, is she a cute little one

Almost one year old today

Baby Chunk is melting away

Yesterday, she was so little

Feeling like I want another

Even if it's way too soon

Very sad to watch her grow up

Every day, a new milestone

Really, really need a baby

Growing Up

I feel like you're bigger today
But that's impossible, there's no way

I just saw you last week
You were barely able to squeak

Your legs look longer and slim
Your face is thinner, less double-chin

Your hands are bigger, and your feet
Your eyes move to the music as if on a beat

You're growing too fast for me
But I can't wait to see who you will be

ABC Baby

Applesauce pouches spilling everywhere
Bottles leaking formula on the couch
Cuddles late at night when nobody can sleep
Dinosaur stuffed animals strewn along the floor
Ever-growing piles of clothes stuffed in the hamper
Feet the size of Post-it notes the smell the size of fish
Giggles sound like ringing bells that toll on bad days
Huggies, Luvs, and Pampers stuffed in every bag
Ice pack frozen for booboos, bumps and scrapes
Jolly jumpers hanging from door frames
King-size bed for mom and dad and dog and sis and babe
Lanolin in every cream that lays around the house
Milk in bags taking over the freezer and the fridge
Naptime for everyone that's home
Onesies of all sizes, shapes and colors
Pacifiers are missing even though they were just here
Quilts stitched with love from grandmas far and near
Rocking chairs that wear a track in the new carpet
Sippy cups with stoppers that seem to not exist
Tiny toes and fingers are the sweetest things
Umbrellas to keep the sun off the little face
Very tired mom and dad
Wet diapers, more and more each day
Xylophone toys constantly make noise
Yellow rubber ducky perfect for a bath
Zip-up sleepers to save our sanity

The shortest hair
The sweetest smell
The smallest hands
The greatest snuggles
The softest skin
The world's best feeling

Rain drops

Splish splash

Wet shoes

Damp socks

Tiny giggles

Belly laughs

Rain coats

Toddler Clothes

Sweet girl

I love most

Baby

Baby
is always
eating.
Diaper is
always dirty.
Baby never seems to
stop crying. I think I'm
going crazy. Baby is so sweet
and snuggly. Baby smells like
the sweetest smells. Powder,
Diapers, formula. Baby makes
me the happiest I will ever be.
Waited so long to hold them,
that I will never take them for
granted. I'll love the cries and
the stinky diapers, I'll love the
things that most moms hate. I'll
love the anxious feelings I get
because at least I'll have them.
I've waited for this moment for
all of my life. To cherish the little
things. So yes, baby cries, and
baby poops, but baby is at
last my own.

I'm Hopeful

Hope for the future is what you bring
You smart little cookie, I love.

Songs of rights and love: I hope you'll sing
My kind-hearted girl, I love.

Strong as any other kid your age or older
My tough little one, I love.

Sharp as a tack, opinionated, bolder
words for your being, I love.

Snippets of women, aunts, grandmas too
Pieces of mommy, I love.

There are so many great things you'll do
I'll always be proud, my love.

Silly Sounds

A cacophony of sounds tumbles from your mouth
Sounds that don't form whole words but parts
Noises that sound like what we want to hear

A mess of syllables chop through the air
These sound almost like words in the whole
Sounds like ma, da, and ba

Now, there are actual words flowing freely
You articulate what you want
I can understand you

I long for the silly sounds
I yearn for the half-words and syllables
I thrive on your complete sentences

Little Boy

this sleeping babe resting on our couch
has brought unimaginable joy
he chuckles loud and mumbles unclear sounds
his smile lights up like a burning candle
even the ones who do not like babies
find him to be the sweetest of loves
he rests here now, and we see him slumber
wondering what his future will hold

Will he become the wisest of doctors
or will he want to stay home instead
should he climb the tallest mountain tops
might he grow taller than you and me
could he be the most well-loved person
what is in store for our little man

Movement

Scooting along the floor
Scooting towards the door
Scooting feels like a chore

Crawling from place to place
Crawling to close the space
Crawling at a fast pace

Pulling up on chairs
Pulling up on stairs
Pulling up while everyone stares

Waddling for a little while
Waddling like it's going out of style
Waddling makes mom smile

Walking far and near
Walking without any fear
Walking and mom cries a tear

Nervous

Excitement swirls all around

New clothes, new shoes, new backpack too

It's almost time to go to school

New friends, new people, and new schedule too

Nerves creep in; what about

Old toys, old games, old naptimes too

Missing mom and dad and brother

Old snacks, old fun, old adventures too

Is time passing more slowly?

The weeks drag on.

Am I really learning?

Class time zooms by.

Is it Christmas yet?

We just had a break.

Can I go back to sleep?

Soon, semesters end.

Alarm clock rings
Roll over to stop it

Ring tone sings
School's calling to say

Stay in bed
No school today

Books to be read
Nothing can top this

Take long naps
And soak up the puppy's kiss

Using new apps
Where'd today go?

Blue

Your eyes are the bluest blue
Some say like the ocean

Your eyes are the bluest blue
Like the snow in the sun

Your eyes are the bluest blue

Piercing as they shine

Your eyes are the bluest blue

Reflecting the color of mine

A Friend

Do friends have to be people
that you've known forever?
Do they even have to be
people you've met?
Can you call someone a friend
if you've known them for days
and never seen their face?

A Dance

A pretty dress
Some fancy shoes
New jewelry too

Some new dress pants
A colored shirt
A matching tie, too

Loud music plays
Sweaty, noisy kids
Lots of laughter, too

Memories made
Good times had
Friendship grew too

Love

Love is the theme of the day
and people always hate it
"I love them every single day"
people like to cry.

I'd like to say that this holiday
is not meant for passing shame
it's not saying that you don't love people
just saying SHOUT IT LOUD.

So next time you celebrate
Valentine's Day, maybe take a break
don't cry out because you hate the day
Shout because of the one who you love this way!

Starry Sky

When gazing upon a midnight sky
you're met with specs of light.
The pictures they make so high above
inspire many things.
The names of them you rarely know
unless you take the time
To marvel at the symmetry
in the shapes of stars aloft.
Orion, a hunter with weapon drawn
the Ursas major and small
A horse, a lion, a scorpion
some without even a name.
You wonder as you look up high
if some stars there are dead
but it doesn't matter because somehow
their light is here and so are you.

Him

His hands are strong like a vice

His scruff is as rough as sandpaper

His heart is like a soft caress

His voice is as deep as the ocean

His eyes pierce like a double-edged sword

His past is like an open book

His words flow like a rushing stream

His hair is like the black of night

His smile is as beautiful as the girl he loves

His thoughts were as curious as a cat

His arms are as strong as a bear

His future is as bright as the sun

His love is as sweet as honey

Houghme

A roommate or two

Strangers I never knew

Became lifelong friends

Because of our school

In weddings and more

What else is in store

For these amazing girls

Who shared a room on a floor

Luggage

You sit in a pile,
Waiting to leave,
To find a new home,
Far away from this place.

You roll to the car,
And throw yourself in,
Wondering where
Life's about to take us.

You ponder anew
How everything fit
Inside one or two
Little bags.

You've been stored
Away in some closet
Finally to be used
Again.

You're great at your job,
You hold things well
Zipped tightly
So you might burst.

You were made for this,
But she wasn't
You're happy for adventure
But it's bittersweet

Vacation

The warm summer sun
with a cooling breeze
time spent on walks
and playing outside
splashing in a creek
freezing cold water
refreshing adventures
distracting from school.

Routine

Classes,
and practice,
and meals,
and work,
and homework,
and meetings,
and naps,
and snacks,
and friends,
and fun,
and sleep

East meets West

While overseas, I met an inspiring man.
He was an imam in the local mosque.
We went to visit, and he came and told us the plan.
Took us inside and shared from his heart.

We learned what is needed for a mosque to be right.
The names of Allah, and Muhammad in script.
The beauty of the artwork was such a cool sight.
To see where he worships was powerful, too.

Young ladies wore headscarves out of respect.
Young men wore long pants and removed their hats.
He sang us a prayer from the Holy Quran.
To bless all our travels as we carried on.

We took photos and left all respectfully dressed.
We weren't disrespectful didn't make a mess.
The imam shared with us outside of the place.
What hurts him about all the stigmas he's faced.

First he shared the real words for Jihad.
A troublesome journey to fulfil one's purpose.
A father's Jihad is to raise his child.
A child's Jihad is to do well in school.

The conversation we had with this man
Is the reason why I'm hurt by our land.
People who act radically aren't tied to a faith
No matter their color or ethnicity.

They simply are radicals who fight for themselves.

Muslims won't support them, and neither do we.
To blame a whole faith for the terror of a few
Is simply, so stupid there's not much to say.

The imam that I met is a Muslim, that's true
But he has no intentions to hurt me or you.
He blessed my friends, myself, and our journey
He's human and hurts just like you and me.

His heart breaks when people misunderstand.
He's overjoyed when it finally makes sense.

He loves sharing and discussing his faith.
Disagreements were peaceful and not filled with shame.

As a foreigner, there in his place of worship
I learned to respect what he had to say
I learned that he and I aren't all that different.
There's just and ocean that separates us.

My life was forever changed by this man
Who willingly taught us and took us by hand.
He prayed without fear and set our minds straight
To the imam, I say thank you and give Romans 8:28.

A Brisk Day

The sun is out and shining brighter now
People walking look like they enjoy it
They laugh and smile and walk together
The weather seems to be enticing
Lots of clusters of people in groups
Life is good here, with lots of chances
To gather our thoughts and enjoy the sun
We walk from class to class to learn more

But there is snow on the ground and in the air
There is more there than some people realize
The wind blows cold and people shiver
Bundled in thick coats warm hats, and long scarves
Boots track in snow and make people shiver
And the sun is shining to lie to our senses

Commencement

You will wake up that day
and walk across the stage.
You will get your degree
and shake many hands.
This day is the one that is
the beginning and the end.

You will move on from
our little world we share.
Our bunked beds and
our cluttered desks.
This place will become
memories as it fades away.

You will be all you can be
and our lives will change.
I'll sleep in an empty room
with no one to talk to in the dark.
I know you will do great things,
but I wonder, could you stay?

In one year,

I'll be married

In one year,

I'll change my name

In one year,

We'll have a party

In one year,

Nothing will be the same!

The birds sang a little louder today
The sun felt a little warmer
The air smelled a little sweeter
My finger felt a little heavier
I'm getting married

With You

I have never felt more in love
than I do with you.
I have never felt more annoyed
than I do with you.
I have never wanted a family more
than I do with you.
I have never been more excited to get married
than I am with you.
I have never wanted to sit in silence
with someone before you.
I have never laughed as much as
I have with you.
I have never cried because I was scared more
than I have over losing you.
I have NEVER loved someone
as much as I love you!

Being Engaged

Is like being alive
But so much
More
Fun.
There's so much to plan,
So much to do before
You finally are tied
Together, forever.
Being engaged
Is like making
Lemonade out of
Lemons because
Of all the stress
That's filled
With love.
Being engaged
Is exciting and hard,
But so rewarding too.

My Husband

My husband's so funny
He's smart, and he's cunning
He loves me the most
For that raise a toast
To my husband, so stunning

Our Wedding Day

A day like no other is this day for me
Love continues to grow between these two
And by the end of today, married we will be

You promise your love will be given to me
I promise my warmth will be only for you
A day like no other is this day for me

No cold feet have come to try and make us flee
With something borrowed, old, new and blue
And by the end of today, married we will be

You hold the lock and I hold the key
To each other's hearts we will be true
A day like no other is this day for me

Our families below us like a mighty tree
Examples of great love flow through
And by the end of today, married we will be

Someday, two may become three
Soft words of love hear us coo
But, a day like no other is this day for me
And by the end of today, married we will be

I finally became an adult!
I can drink.
I pay bills.
I make dinner.
I go to work.
I do laundry.
I do dishes.
I sweep.
I take out the trash.
I have finally become an adult....
Can I go back to being a kid?

M y best friend
A nnoying each other for life
R ings on each other's hand
R eaching the tall cupboards
I ce cream dates just for us
A cting like there's nothing wrong
G etting upset at silly things
E xciting adventures still await

Infertile

Nobody said it would be difficult

I always assumed it would come easy

That's what I get for assuming I guess

It's hard, it sucks, I can't do it again

I have always wanted a big family

But this first baby is taking so long

I don't even know if that's possible

I just want to snuggle sweet baby cheeks

And smell the sweet smell of the newborn's hair

My body aches for something it can't have

While I watch others around me get it

I have hope that someday, this pain will leave

On the day when I can snuggle my own

For now, I look on with envy of them

Loss

Even the way she stands hurts
A simple hand at the heart
Seems so gentle until you see
She's holding herself together

Her eyes seem empty, and they are
She's lost the one who meant the most
She's drowning in the guilt
She survived and the little one did not

People talk like she isn't there
The words cut like a knife
She didn't mean for the baby to die
No matter what people say

Everyone blames her
Because she was home
The more they say it
The more it seems true

Now she's trapped
With thoughts spinning round
Was it really her fault
And she is lost

You won't pull her back
Was there something
She could have done
The guilt overwhelms

Hair disheveled and clothes dark
She mourns the loss
Of the baby's first
And then for herself

Counting On

One tiny child is running off to bed
Two happy parents ready for some sleep
Three big dogs are watching out together
Four quiet fish swim gently in their bowl
Five dirty dishes sitting in the sink
Six meals are in the fridge, ready to eat
Seven warm blankets on the bedroom floor
Eight hours of sleep for even mom and dad
Nine different choices for breakfast today
Ten o'clock, time to go, or we'll be late
Eleven happy family members wait
Twelve more days to take a break sounds just great
Thirteen little grandkids have all played here
Fourteen weeks, along with the newest one

The First Day

On the very first day
of kindergarten you
could not wait until
high school.

On the very first day
of high school
college seemed like
a dream.

On the very first day
of college classes
blurred and you
wanted to work.

On the very first day
of the rest of
your life you
sat and thought...

What comes next?

Grandparenting

Grandchildren running about the house

Running so fast I can barely keep up

Older children play on their phones

While parents sit around and chat

I never imagined I'd find myself here

Not really sure how the time flew so fast

Great-grandchildren will fill our home soon

Only one, but more will come

Later in the evening, I find myself tired

Dreading the work it takes to clean up

Everyone has gone home; the house is quiet

Ready for them to come back.

You're Crazy Too

Over the cuckoo's warm nest, one bird flew.
Outside of the nest, the cuckoos all play.
Not everyone thinks that you're crazy, too.

We lose ourselves a little; that's too true.
Doing our lives in our own special way.
Over the cuckoo's warm nest, one bird flew.

The lack of care is the world's biggest clue.
Keeping the feelings of hurting at bay
Not everyone thinks that you're crazy, too.

Emotions and feelings begin to brew.
Mundane things that are your hurdles today.
Over the cuckoo's warm nest, one bird flew.

From your past experiences, they drew,
the hard things that started to make you fray.
Not everyone thinks that you're crazy, too.

This is the moment that somehow you knew,
The place you're in didn't want you to stay.
Over the cuckoo's barren nest, you flew,
but everyone knows that you're crazy, too.

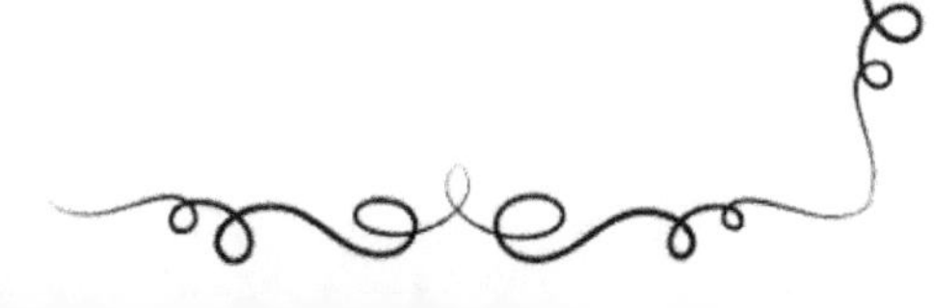

Christmastime

Christmas time is here.
With lights and trees, all strung about the town.
The cookies are baked and ready to eat.
The presents are wrapped with care.
The stockings are hung on the stairs, waiting to be filled with cheer.
Christmas plans are being made as the kids look towards their break.
Mom and dad are happy, too, to have a couple of days.
Grandma and Grandpa are ready to spoil the kids with candy toys and other sweets too.
We'll see cousins and friends and celebrate together.
No matter what comes, we will always remember that the reason we get together is that long ago, in a town called Bethlehem, a mom had a baby who would come to save the whole world.

My body aches, it does

Spry and young and fit, I was

Now old and gray and slow

That life I used to know

Just memories of youth that 'twas

Memories

Memories kept
in the sound of a voice
in the look on a face

Memories kept
in a passing thought
in the tears on a cheek

Memories kept
in the way a dad walks
in the way that he smiles

Memories kept
of a hard-working grandpa
of a kind-hearted grandma

Memories kept
in a piece of his suit
in a piece of her dress

Confidence

She holds her head up high
her body follows suit
she stand up tall
squares her hips
and no one bothers her

She slouches down
slinks into herself
she's never looked so sad
her body sags
and people notice too

Today

Today I was assaulted
by the song of singing birds

The chirps the tweets are
songs of spring
but it's winter

Today this assault
made me a little sad
because the birds don't know

It's winter still
you may yet freeze
be careful, little bird

A Mess

Oops! She shrieks
as she drops
the pan, full of
dinner
no back-up plan.

She sobs as he
come through the door
herself and the
food
piled on the floor.

His gentle embrace
and warm kiss
these moments she
swears
are pure bliss

A Different You

I never knew what it would
be like to go back as
who I am.

It was different, hard and
felt brand new to be
there again.

I've never been there before
at least not this version
of me.

It felt weird, unique
and I love it still as
a part of my story.

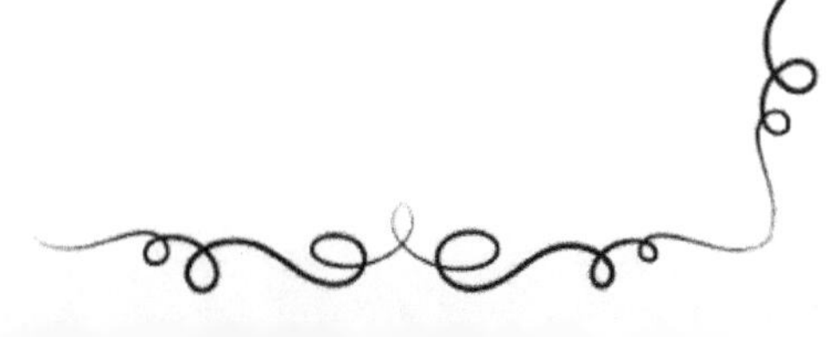

To My Dad

If ever there was
a job that time
has simply forgot.
A pastor would be
that one that suffered
from that lot.

Tireless work from
dawn till dusk
every day of the week.
Don't pay his wages
for time served he
must turn the other cheek

Interest rises so
do the wages of
Tom, Dick, or Joe.
But the same work
brings less money
no raises here to show.

Our pastor dear, time has
lost and left his wallet
empty.

Resolutions

"New Year, New Me"
They cry from rooftops,
on Facebook, and secretly.

What is so wrong with
who you are? Do you
have to change? Is
this day the only
time for reinventing?

For this year, I'll be
more active, I'll sleep
better, I'll drink less,
smoke less, change.

For this year, I will
do what I say for
3 days, get bored,
and go back to who
I am.

This New Year, you'll
see me as who I've
always been

The Color Blue

It's the color you feel
when you're a little
too cold.

The one when there's
sadness with a touch
of joy.

The color of cold
water rushing down
your throat.

The color that's behind
your eyes as you grieve
and cry.

AFR

Your silent laugh as you look at things
that seem funny to only you
makes everyone else around you smile
for reasons no one knows

The thirst you have for learning more
even when it's not easy
is inspiring to everyone you meet
for reasons no one knows

Sometimes, the teenage years
begin to take their toll
you seem different than the girl we knew
for reasons no one knows

You will make your choices to grow up
you'll choose a good career
You will be you, and that's the truth
for reasons no one knows

Fear

If my legs stopped working, I'm sure I would too
Imagine the things that I couldn't do
couldn't walk for one,
couldn't run for two

I'd be in a wheelchair and half my height
No more running to fly a kite
I couldn't get into my house
My life just wouldn't feel right

I couldn't be in my favorite places
I'd miss out on familiar faces
Not climbing stairs
Or running races

My mind would be very dark
The shock putting out any spark
I'd ask for help
Caged like a lark

Couldn't cook on a stovetop
Couldn't pick up what I dropped
No jumps on a couch
No belly flops

ELR

My heart breaks when I hear you say
Things that put you down
Everyone knows those words aren't true
Except for you, sweet girl
It will take time to understand
You are made in the image of God
But for now, trust me, I know it's hard
You can be who you want to be
Be brave, be kind, be strong and dance
Let your passions show you how
To be the woman you're meant to be
I believe in all you are

Someday

He'll grow into those shoes
Someday
He'll walk straighter
Someday
He'll wear the hat better
Someday
He'll dress himself
Someday

He's learning so much
Today
He's laughing at things
Today
He's making fun faces
Today
He's growing up
Today

He was so little
Yesterday
He was crawling, not walking
Yesterday
He was drinking a bottle
Yesterday
He was nothing but flutters
Yesterday

MPT

Her hair has gotten longer

she has gotten taller

when she laughs, she's beautiful

I wish I knew when it happened

she's brilliant, and she's loopy

but the perfect mix of both

she's learned to cook

she cleans the house

I wish I stopped and watched

she's in high school now

I've lost some time

not too much, I hope

I'll be more intent on watching her grow

my dearest girl.

Never Ending

A list of things a mile long
that you need to do
the power goes out
you start to think
what can I get done

Laundry needs water
which is moved
by electricity
no drying clothes
or washing anything

With no water comes
a list that is longer still
of things that can't
be done today
they seem more important now

Dishes, showers, cooking food,
walking around at night,
charging things like laptops,
phones, opening the fridge,
watching movies, hearing the radio

It looks like you must settle
for snuggling on the couch
grab a blanket, book and drink
keep warm and don't get bored
read with love you have always had

The power will come back
but only when you decide
this day without electricity
you do not want to end
thoughts like that turn lights back on

Suspense

We sit in wait and grow anxious
There are four of us here
The hymn dies down, and the music fades
The time is drawing near

Scripture is read, and our hearts flutter
He stands up from his chair
His words flow smoothly with no breaks
Use all of us; it is fair

He mentions that he has a tale
He picked it up this week
I was not home at all I am safe
My sisters squeek

The child picked this up at school
He states with confidence
She counsels those who need her help
Two left in solemness

He got it from his math class
Now we are all confused
He continues his recounting
None of us were used

We glance around bewildered
We wonder furiously
A little voice calls from the back
"Pop Pop, Seriously?"

ZDR

Every day is different

But he is always the same

He sees me and his eyes light up

His hugs are the greatest squeeze

He knows the days I need him most

Those ones, he is sweeter than the rest

The love I feel from his little heart

Is the best thing I understand

This time of shameless hugs

Runs short as he grows

My sweet little bug

I love you more than most

CAR

His smile is an impish one
it always makes me wonder
what could he be up to
and does he need a partner
he sneaks around the house
his giggle ringing loud
running from the emptiness
until he is tired out
he will not stop his playtime
unless it is time to leave
then he crawls up on the couch
and cuddles next to me
my sweet nephew has me
right where he needs
I would give him anything
he just whispers please

Sabbath

7 AM on Saturday
Most everyone is asleep
A small group of people stirs
Ready for the day's adventure

Morning brings out the music
Chimes and a choir
Songs for the day played
Musicians of all ages

Time flies to sabbath school
High school students
Not really listening
Absorbed in something else

Worship hour in the church
Quiet whispers from the back pews
Pastor's sermon hits home
Hymns and scripture, too

Fellowship time with everyone
Laughs hugs and stories
Old with young ones
All part of a family

Naps await at home
The day of rest is blessed
Sleep and love together
The Lord himself is true

Valentines

Kindergarten kids exchange cards
they love and love almost everyone
mom said everyone gets one
there is little complaint from these

High School comes, and teens shake it off
love's not cool to show and cards are lame
unless, of course, there's a girl in play
what she likes he likes, even love

Dating years with college around
been together for three whole years
done with flowers and chocolate
what will she use the most that's the best gift

The day has come around again
celebrated many years now
a ring is what she'd love to see
so down to a knee he asks

Married life is such a joy
does there really need to be just one day
she's loved always and so is he
presents can't mean more than words

Fifty years of growing old
loving more and more each day
the gifts don't mean so much
as long as he stays here with her.

He's gone now, and she is sad
but the feelings shared are still around
this day is such a special one
she feels him most on this day of love

Syruping

Heavy footsteps in the snow,

sloshing buckets emptied,
wafts of exhaust and smokey smells

of the hot wood stove,
The sound of rolling, bubbling, boiling.

Scratchy filters and smooth, hard buckets.

Steam and a sickeningly sweet smell.

Finally, the red line rises. Bottles filled,

seals and stickers cling,

ready for the breakfasts on tables everywhere.

ACT

The eldest one seems so strong.

Inside, she's torn apart.

She's always been the tough one.

It's ripped at her heart.

She's gone to school

Worked three jobs

She's never quite at rest

But soon she'll know

The greatest love

With arms wrapped around

And peace

The Creek

I've seen the creek a million times
but never through your eyes.
It never held the interest
it does for kids your size.

The running water,
the cobbled stones,
the moss, grass and mud.

Things I've always noticed
I'm sure, but never
like you did.

The way you hold
each little rock,
like precious gold
and squeal at little fish.

Things I'd never thought
to care for until
you showed me.

The creek, the world
everything.
It's different
with you here.

Being your mom,
my greatest joy.
I'm learning
with you here.

Printed in the USA
CPSIA information can be obtained
at www.ICGtesting.com
CBHW080459281124
18091CB00035B/1450